CAMBRIDGE SKILLS FOR FLUENCY
Series Editor: Adrian Doff

Writing 2

Andrew Littlejohn

CAMBRIDGE
UNIVERSITY PRESS

CAMBRIDGE UNIVERSITY PRESS
Cambridge, New York, Melbourne, Madrid, Cape Town, Singapore, São Paulo

Cambridge University Press
The Edinburgh Building, Cambridge CB2 2RU, UK

www.cambridge.org
Information on this title: www.cambridge.org/9780521367578

First published 1991
9th printing 2005

Printed in the United Kingdom at the University Press, Cambridge

A catalogue record for this publication is available from the British Library

ISBN-13 978-0-521-36757-8
ISBN-10 0-521-36757-3

Contents

Map of the book

Unit	Aspects of writing	Structures	Functions	Vocabulary areas
1 The good life	Idea maps; questionnaires; reports; paragraphs.	Present simple; reported speech.	Reporting; describing places.	Work conditions; life situation.
2 Time to spare	Week plans; notes to a paragraph; revising; poems.	Present simple; past simple; question forms.	Describing hobbies.	Personal activities; hobbies.
3 *A photo album	Comments on photos; notes to a paragraph.	Present and past simple; present continuous; question forms.	Describing scenes; describing activities.	Family relation-ships; verbs of the senses; verbs of action.
4 Are you free?	Letters of invitation and acceptance.		Inviting; accepting; declining.	Social occasions; visits; celebrations.
5 Food, glorious food	Listing; menu; reviews; paragraphs.	Adjectives; past simple and continuous.	Describing food; describing a scene.	Dishes; ingredients; cooking terms; kitchens.
6 For sale	Word maps; small ads; notes to a paragraph.	Adjectives; past simple.	Advertising; describing domestic objects.	Adjectives; category words.
7 Please read carefully	Signs; instructions.	Imperatives; prepositions.	Giving instructions.	Furniture and rooms; domestic activities.
8 Holiday time	Advice leaflets; posters; notes to a paragraph.	Imperatives; present simple.	Giving advice; persuading.	Holidays.
9 A learning workshop	Needs/wants charts; notes; devising exercises.	Can/could you.	Getting help while learning.	Learning English.
10 Lifetimes	CVs; graphs; notes to a paragraph.	Past tenses; present tenses.	Describing your past life.	CVs; stages in life.

* Students will need to bring their own photographs to class for some of the activities in this unit.

Unit	Aspects of writing	Structures	Functions	Vocabulary areas
11 Write soon	Greetings cards; personal letters.	Present perfect; past tenses; present tense.	Greetings; giving news.	Greetings card messages; personal news.
12 What's it for?	Descriptions; paragraphs.	'for' + gerund; 'if' sentences.	Describing uses; describing objects.	Verbs of action; common objects.
13 Puzzle time	Word puzzles; crosswords; paragraphs.		Describing a scene.	Verbs of action.
14 Describing people	Descriptions; notes to a paragraph.	Present tenses; past simple; 'used to'.	Describing people.	Physical descriptions of people; childhood activities.
15 Looking at writing	Fluent v. accurate writing; checklists of common mistakes.	Common mistakes.		
16 The Earth is . . .	Notes; notes to a paragraph; revising; dialogues; poems.	Present tenses; question forms.	Expressing wishes; describing countries.	Descriptions of countries.
17 Body talk	Paragraphs.	Present and future tenses.	Explaining meaning of gestures; interpreting meanings.	Gestures; body language; personal descriptions.
18 Writing for yourself	Notes, reminders, plans; diary entries; paragraphs.	Past tenses; present tenses; adjectives.	Describing a day; describing your life situation.	Daily events.
19 Look after yourself	A first aid leaflet; questionnaires.	Imperatives; question forms.	Instructions.	First aid; daily routines; factors affecting your health.
20 The real you	Preparing questions; a story.	Past tenses; present tenses.	Giving personal information; describing a woodland scene.	Personal information; woodlands.

For my mother and the memory of my father.

Acknowledgements

Many thanks to:

Jeanne McCarten, Alison Silver, Kendall Clarke, Lindsay White and everybody at Cambridge University Press for making the book possible;

Peter Ducker, Chris Evans, Cathy Hall, Lisa Hall, Helen Herbert, Leslie Marshall, Clyde Pearson, Nigel Westwood and Shaun Williams for their skills in art and design;

Adrian Doff, Bella McEvoy and members of the Teaching of Writing group at the University of Lancaster, for their perceptive comments on the pilot edition;

and, most important of all, Lita, Daniel and Fiona for their continual patience and support and for the smiles on their faces.

The author and publishers would like to thank all the institutions who helped pilot the material.

The author and publishers are grateful to the following for permission to reproduce photographs:
Telegraph Colour Library (p. 7 top left, top right, bottom right, p. 9 top left, p. 56 d, e); J. Allan Cash (p. 7 bottom left, p. 8, p. 9 top right, middle right, bottom right, p. 45 b); Barnaby's Picture Library (p. 9 middle left); Sally and Richard Greenhill Photographers Photo Library (p. 9 bottom left, p. 57 e); Format Photographers (p. 10 top left, Maggie Murray; top right, Brenda Prince; bottom right, Judy Harrison); Rex Features Ltd (p. 45 a, c, f); Syndication International (p. 45 d, e).

The photographs on p. 10 (bottom left), p. 45, p. 56 (top left, a, b, c), p. 57 (a, b, c, f) were taken by Jeremy Pembrey. The photograph on p. 57 (d) was taken by Andrew Littlejohn.

Drawings by Chris Evans, Lisa Hall, Helen Herbert, Leslie Marshall, Clyde Pearson and Shaun Williams. Artwork by Peter Ducker, Cathy Hall, Hardlines and Wenham Arts.
Book design by Peter Ducker MSTD.

Introduction to students

Writing 2 contains lots of different activities to help you learn English. Some of these will help you with writing itself but most of them will help you learn English generally, through writing.

The book is full of choices. You can do the units in any order and you don't have to do everything in each unit. (The units at the beginning of the book are a little easier than the units at the end and, usually, the first activities in a unit are the easiest.) If you want to practise a particular thing, look at the *Map of the book* on pages iv–v. That will tell you which unit it is in.

There are answers for some of the exercises at the back of the book. Usually, these answers are only examples of what you *could* write and your own answers may be very different. Exercises with answers have a symbol, like this: ⚷

For many of the activities in this book, you have to work with someone. Sometimes you will write something as a pair or a small group and then give it to some other students. Sometimes you will write something by yourself and then compare it with your neighbour. The point of this is not just to write, but to talk about writing. In this way, you will improve not only your writing but your general knowledge of English as well.

We hope you learn a lot from this book and enjoy using it.

1 | The good life

1 What is 'the good life' to you? Work in pairs and make some notes, like this:

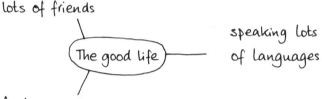

Here are some ideas:

holidays   social life   salary   house(s)   food   family
car   drink   friends   home   clothes   children

When you are ready, compare with the other students in your class. Do you all agree?

2 What about 'a good job'? What is a good job to you? This time, work in a small group and make some more notes:

a good job

interesting

nice people to work with

no pressure

Now, in your group, use your notes to make a questionnaire. Like this:

	agree	don't know	disagree
1 My job is interesting.	☐	☐	☐
2 I work with nice people.	☐	☐	☐
3 I don't have any pressure at work.	☐	☐	☐
4	☐	☐	☐

(If you are still at school or college, write about student life.)

When you are ready, each person in your group should interview one or two other people in the class (or outside the class) and tell the others in the group what he/she found out. Then, in your group, write a report. Like this:

Most people said that their job is interesting but only a few said they worked with nice people. About half of the people said that they did not have any pressure at work.

Here are some useful words:

everybody   nearly all the people   most people
about half of the people   only a few   nobody

3 'The good life' is more than a good job. *Where* would you like to live? Close your eyes and imagine that you are there. What can you see? Note down your answers to these questions:

Where is your dream house?
What does it look like?
What can you see from the windows?
Is there a garden? What is in it?
What else can you see or hear?

Now, using your notes, write a paragraph about your dream house. Add any points as they come into your head. This, for example, is what I can see. Where do you think the house is?

My house is by the sea. It is a very large white house with big rooms and fans in the ceilings. From my bedroom window I can see the hills and the open sea. I have a small garden with banana trees, mangos and palm trees. There's also a parrot that says 'Buenos dias' when it sees me. From the bottom of my garden I can walk to the beach.

When you are ready, give your paragraph to someone else in your class to read. Can they guess where your dream house is?

2 | Time to spare

1 Imagine that you have one week of extra holiday and you can do all the things that you never usually have time to do. What would you do? Make a chart like the one below.

	Monday	Tuesday	Wednesday	Thursday	Friday	Saturday	Sunday
morning	sleep!	stay in bed and read a book					
afternoon	tidy up the cupboard in the hall	go shopping					
evening	do the ironing and watch TV	write some letters					

Compare your chart with other people in your class. Do most people have a lot of work to do or do they want to relax?

2 What is your main hobby or special interest? Make some notes about it, like this:

Playing the guitar

- classical music and folk songs

- started when I was 18

- don't play very much now

- a new guitar?

Now, in a small group, use your notes to tell other students about it.

3 Write a short paragraph about your hobby or interest. Use your notes from
Exercise 2 to help you and leave extra space between each line. Like this:

My main hobby is playing the guitar. I usually play classical

music but I can also play some folk songs. I started to

play about 20 years ago when I was 18 years old. I don't

play as much now as before because I don't have a lot

of time to spare. I would like to buy a new guitar soon

but a good guitar can cost hundreds of pounds.

While you are writing, compare with other students in your class. See if there
are any ways to improve what you have written.

When you are ready, give your paragraph to another student to read. Read the
paragraph that you receive and add some questions that you would like to
know more about. For example:

What songs can you play?
Where do the best guitars come from?
How long did it take you to learn?

When you get your paper back, see if you can put the answers to the questions
into your paragraph. Like this:

My main hobby is playing the guitar. I usually play classical
       such as 'Guantanamera' and songs by Paul Simon
music but I can also play some folk songs. I started to
                              and I'm still learning
play about 20 years ago when I was 18 years old. I don't

play as much now as before because I don't have a lot

of time to spare. I would like to buy a new guitar soon

but a good guitar can cost hundreds of pounds.
The best guitars come from Spain, but there are also
good guitars from Japan.

When you are ready, pass your paragraph back to the person who wrote the
questions.

4 Time to spare can be different things to different people. Below are three poems that different people have written. Where do you think each person was when they wrote their poem? What were they doing? How did they feel?

Time to spare
I can feel the sun on my back
And hear the waves
I can hear the children shouting
Happy that they are alive
Happy that we are together
With so much
Time to spare.

Time to spare
Between trains
But so much to do
Another difficult day
How I hate the pressure
The clock is ticking
I'm wasting my time, writing
And now there's no
Time to spare.

Time to spare
There's no one else here
Only me and the cat
A very fat cat
He's got so much to spare
That's nothing new
Me
I'm nervous
Soon, perhaps, she'll ring
But what shall I do now
With so much
Time to spare?

Think of (or imagine) a time when you had some time to spare (perhaps waiting for a train or bus or to see the doctor). Write a poem about it. You could write about:

– where you are
– what you are waiting for
– what you can see or hear
– how you feel

Try to start and end the poem with the words 'Time to spare'. When you have finished, read out your poem to the rest of the class, if you would like to.

3 | A photo album

1   Do you have any photographs of your family or friends? In a small group, pass
your photographs around. Note down any questions that you would like to ask
about the photographs.

Is this your daughter?

Why are you dressed like that?

How long ago was this photo taken?

Was it taken in your home town?

When you have passed them all around, talk about each person's photograph.
Use the questions you noted down.

2

Write a few sentences about your photograph on a piece of paper. (They can be about the same photos you looked at in Exercise 1 or about a new photograph.) Say what is happening in the photograph. Like this:

This is me skiing with my daughter in France! We were there for two weeks last year. It was our first time skiing and we were very tired most of the time, as you can see. I wasn't very good at it – I think I spent most of the time on the ground! Skiing is very difficult but I would like to try it again sometime. It was really beautiful up in the mountains and so quiet. It was fantastic to be above the clouds.

When you are ready, pin all the photographs on the classroom wall and mix up the pieces of paper on a table. Choose a paper and read it. Can you find the correct photograph?

3

Here are some more photographs, this time of places and situations. Imagine that you are in one of the photos. Note down your answers to these questions:

Where are you?   What can you see, hear or smell?
What are you doing?   How are you feeling?

Find out what your neighbour imagined.
Now write a paragraph about your ideas. Like this:

I'm sitting on the grass, up here in the hills. In the distance, I can hear voices. They sound like children playing somewhere. I'm thinking about how beautiful it is here and how much I would like to live in the countryside. It's so peaceful and the air is fresh and clean. I feel very happy and I really don't want to go back to my house in the city.

When you have finished, find another student in your class who wrote about
the same photograph. Compare what you wrote.

4 These are rather strange photographs. The most important parts are missing! What do you think each person is doing? Where do you think they are? What is happening? What has just happened? Choose two or three pictures and write a paragraph about each one. Like this:

I think this boy is throwing something. He is looking down to the ground, so perhaps he is trying to hit something. He is probably outside in the park playing with a ball with some friends. I think he's singing a song at the same time or saying something, because he has got his mouth open. It's not very cold outside, because he has only got a shirt on.

When you are ready, read out what you wrote to the rest of the class. Listen to what other students wrote and then look in the *Answer key* to see who was right.

4 | Are you free?

1 Here are some invitations and some replies. Can you match them up?

a)

Dear Grandma,

How are you? We haven't heard from you for a long time.

We are going to stay at home all summer. Why don't you come and visit us? We would love to see you.

All the best,

b)

21st Dec

Dear Andy,

Thanks for the invitation. I'm afraid we're going away for the New Year. I'll give you a ring when we get back.

Perhaps we can come and visit in February.

Love

Kh

c)

Mr and Mrs Brown
request the pleasure of the company of

Mr + Mrs T. Roscow

at the marriage
of their daughter, Susan, to Mr Steven Jones
on March 16th, 1992 at 10.30a.m.
at Hindley Town Hall
and afterwards at
The Globe Hotel, Ashleigh.

R.S.V.P.

d)

17 Hayton Rd
Horwich

Feb. 13th

Dear Mr and Mrs Brown,

Thank you very much for your kind invitation to Susan's wedding. We are very happy to accept.

Yours sincerely,

e)

27 East Rd
Totnes
Dec. 17th

Dear Tom and Diana,

Just a short note to say we're having a party on New Year's Eve and we were wondering if you could come. We have lots of space so there's no problem about staying the night.

Anyway, let us know soon.
Love,

f)

16 Prospect St
Warrington
15th June

Dear Nigel,

Thank you very much for your kind letter. I would love to come and visit you. The first week of July would be best for me. I can come by train. Is that all right for you?

All my love,

Which invitation and reply are the most formal? Why do you think so?

2 Look at the letters in Exercise 1 again. Can you find phrases to do each of the following? Write them down.

to open a letter   to close a letter
to say thank you   to say yes to something
to suggest something   to say no to something
to invite somebody

3 Invite somebody! Work in pairs. Choose one thing from each of the boxes below to write a letter of invitation.

— **What?** —

- You are going on a holiday to Sevilla, Spain. You want to invite someone to come with you.

- You are going on holiday. You want to invite someone to live in your house (they can look after the cat).

- You think of something!

- You are going to a new restaurant for the first time. You want to invite someone to eat there.

- It is your birthday. You want to invite someone to your party.

— **When?** —

March 24th — March 16th — March 30th — March 18th

— **How long?** —

one night — the weekend — 1 week — 2 weeks

Send your letter to *two* other pairs. See Exercises 1 and 2 for help with what to say. Lay your letter out like this:

> *your address*
> *date*
>
> Dear . . .
>
> How are you? . . .
>
> We're . . . and we were wondering if . . .
> *or* We're . . . Would you like to . . . ?
> *or* We're . . . Why don't you . . . ?
>
> . . . .
>
> *your name*

Read the letters you get. Decide which one you can say 'yes' to and which one you have to say 'no' to (check the dates). Write short letters back to the pairs you get the letters from, like this:

```
                                        your address
                                        date


   Dear . . .

   Thank you very much for the invitation to . . .

      I would love to . . .
or    I'm afraid . . .

      . . . . . . . .

   your name
```

4 **Write another 'thank you' letter, this time with the whole class.**

Copy the phrases below on to a piece of paper leaving plenty of space after each line. Write a name after 'Dear' (perhaps someone in the class or a famous person). Fold the paper over at the top and pass it on. Complete the next sentence on the paper that you receive (you can write anything you like) and then fold it over and pass it on. Continue until you finish all the sentences. Pass the papers on twice more, open them up and read out your letter to the class!

```
Dear ...

Just a note to say thanks very much for ...

It was ...

I ...

I hope ...

Anyway, ...

Best wishes,
```

5 | Food, glorious food

1 Here are some dishes from different countries of the world. Can you match the countries with the names of the dishes?

Spain	tacos
Mexico	fondue
Italy	curry
India	roast beef and Yorkshire pudding
England	paella
Switzerland	spaghetti bolognese
Germany	sausage and sauerkraut

What is in each dish? Choose one or two dishes and write a list of the ingredients. (You can check in the *Answer key*.)

2 What dishes do you eat in your country? Think of one or two and write a list of their ingredients. Do not write the name of the dish.

?

milk
flour
eggs

?

Gruyère cheese
Emmenthal cheese
Kirsch

?

chillies
beef
onion
tomatoes
kidney beans

When you are ready, put all your papers together and mix them up. Choose one. Do you know what dish it is and/or where it comes from?

3 Unfortunately, food is not always nice to eat! Here are some words to describe it. Divide the words into three columns – one column for *good* qualities, one for *bad* qualities and one for qualities that can be *good or bad*.

burnt	cold	greasy	soft	sweet	delicious
fresh	stale	warm	salty	overcooked	raw
hard	tasty	hot	tough	tender	undercooked

good	bad	good or bad
tasty	stale	hot

Compare your columns with your neighbour's.

4 Work in pairs.
You are opening a new restaurant.
Plan your menu for the first night.
You want to serve some special dishes.

When you are ready, pass your menu to two other pairs. They are your first customers.

Look at the menus that you receive. You have just eaten at a new restaurant. Decide if the dishes were good or bad and then write a review for each one.

The chicken was tough. The carrots were too salty. The potatoes were undercooked. The ...
The fish was excellent! The meat was tender and ...

When you are ready, give your review to the pair who gave you the menu. Read the reviews that you receive. Was *your* first night a success?

5 Restaurants are not always as they should be . . .
Imagine that you are a health inspector. Recently, you went to visit a very expensive restaurant. You went in and you saw the kitchen on page 17 . . .

What did you see? With a partner, first decide what is wrong with the kitchen. These words may be useful:

a cigarette   beetles   dirty dishes   a rat
a chef's hat   cigarette ends

Find out what other people in your class thought.

Now, by yourself, write about what you saw, like this:

The kitchen was disgusting. There were dirty plates everywhere and ...

While you are writing, look at what other students have written. See if there are any ways you can improve what you have written.

6 | For sale

1 How can you describe things for sale? Work with a partner. Choose one of the names of things listed below and make a word map. Like this:

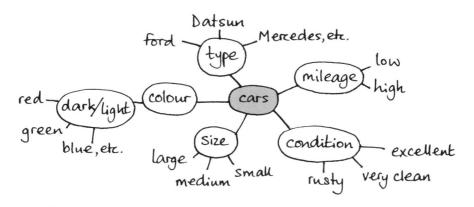

houses   clothes   food   bus/train services   books   furniture
hi-fi equipment   computers   watches/clocks

Compare your word map with another pair who have chosen the same thing. Then look at other students' word maps. Have they written down any words which are new to you?

2 Recently, you saw an advertisement in a newspaper. This is what it said:

> **1988 Renault 5.** Beautiful condition, very little rust, good tyres, one careful owner, radio and aerial, electric windows, comfortable leather seats, low mileage. £4,495.

But this is what the car looked like:

Write a correct advertisement for the car, like this:

FOR SALE: Renault 5. Terrible condition. Lots of rust. ...

3 Look at the things below. What information would you find about each one in an advertisement? Discuss it with the rest of the class.

Now imagine that you want to sell one of the things on page 19. Work with a partner, choose one and write an advertisement for it. Try to make it sound attractive.

When you have finished, exchange advertisements with another pair of students. Imagine that you went to see what they wanted to sell. How was it? Use your imagination.

First, underline or make a note of the points in the advertisement. Add any other points you would like to make.

Bicycle. 26" wheels, 10 gears, almost new,
two new <u>tyres</u>, side <u>bags</u>, many <u>extras</u>.

– one of the tyres wasn't new
– no chain
– the brakes
– no bell
– extras: an old bell, a pump, a can of oil

Then write a paragraph about it. Try to join the points together, like this:

The bicycle was in a terrible condition. The seat was completely broken and the bags were old and dirty. It didn't have a chain, the brakes didn't work very well and one of the tyres <u>wasn't</u> new. There weren't 'many extras', only an old bell, a pump and a can of oil.

When you have finished, give your paragraph to the pair who wrote the advertisement.

7 | Please read carefully

1 Here are some common objects or situations. What instructions would you expect to find on each one? Make a list of your ideas. For example:

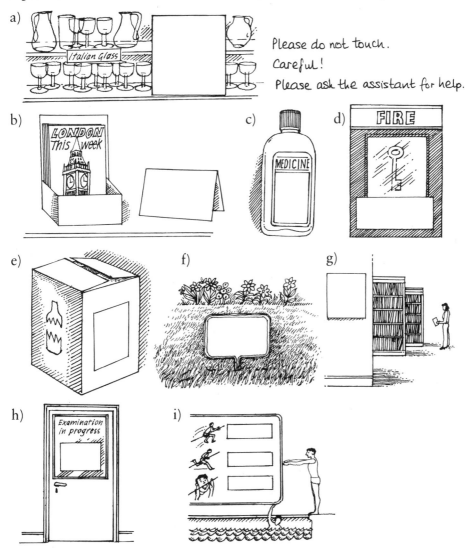

a)

Italian Glass

Please do not touch.
Careful!
Please ask the assistant for help.

b) LONDON This week

c) MEDICINE

d) FIRE

e)

f)

g)

h) Examination in progress

i)

Compare your ideas with other students in your class.

2

Look at the illustrations below. How can you describe the position of the bookcase in each one? (There are two or three possible ways for some of them.)

next to   between   behind   at the top/bottom of   against
in front of   near   on the left/right   in the corner

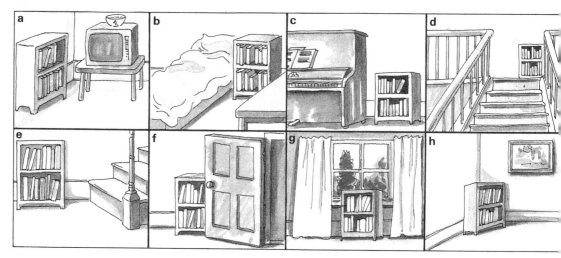

On Plan A opposite, draw in the furniture anywhere you want, but try not to let anyone else see. Then write down *exact* instructions for someone to put the furniture in the same places as you. For example:

*Put the table in bedroom 1, on the left, next to the big window.
Put the bookcase in the hall near the front door against the
living room wall.*

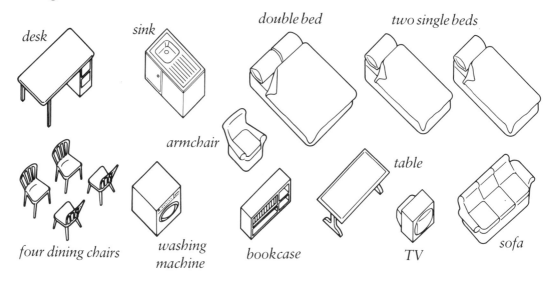

desk   sink   double bed   two single beds

armchair   table

four dining chairs   washing machine   bookcase   TV   sofa

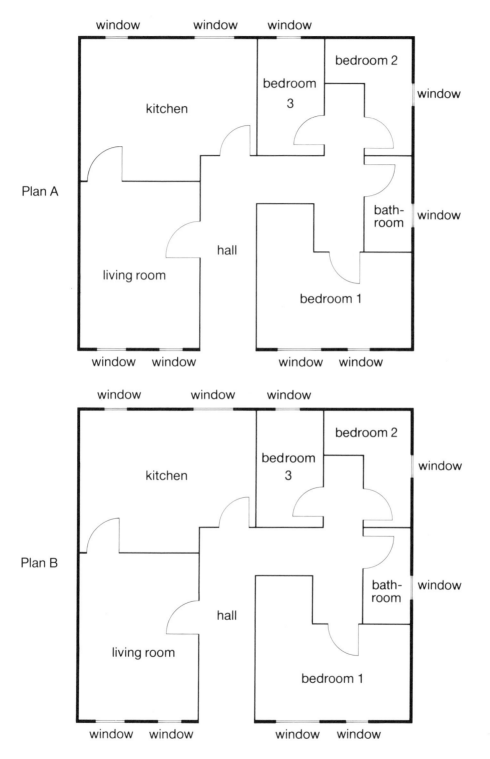

Plan A

Plan B

When you are ready, exchange instructions with another student. Follow the instructions that you receive and draw the symbols on Plan B. Check with the other student's Plan A to see if you are right!

3 Robots . . . the dream of the future. A robot that can do all the housework is a fantastic idea, but is it possible? Robots are very stupid. You have to programme them to do what you want.

In a small group, think of something that you have to do at home. Make some notes about what you have to do and then write down *exact* instructions for doing it. Use your dictionary to help you. For example:

<u>Washing up</u>

Turn on the taps and fill the sink with warm water. Add some washing-up liquid and then take a dirty plate and put it in the water. Clean the plate with a brush and then take it out of the water. Put it on the side to drain and then dry it with a cloth.

Here are some activities:

laying the table	cooking some food	lighting a cigarette
cleaning your shoes	making the bed	using the telephone
cleaning the windows	opening a tin	making a cup of coffee

When you are ready, ask someone from another group to be your 'robot'. Read out your instructions. The 'robot' has to mime them exactly. Are your instructions clear and full?

8 | Holiday time

1 Imagine that you are working in a travel agency and you have to produce a leaflet for people travelling around the world. What advice would you give them? Work with your neighbour and make lists of things to take and things to do before they go and while they are travelling.

> ## AROUND THE WORLD   Advice to Travellers
>
> *Things to take*   *Before you go*   *While you are travelling*
>
> passport   make your flight   be careful where you eat
>   reservations

When you have finished, find out what other people in your class thought. Which things do you think are the most important?

2 Some people go to very unusual places on holiday. There are some examples below. Why do you think people might go there? What can they do there? Discuss each one with the others in your class and note down some ideas.

A LIGHTHOUSE   THE AMAZON JUNGLE   THE ANTARCTIC   THE SAHARA DESERT

Now work with your neighbour and, using your notes, write a few sentences
for a poster to advertise a holiday in each place. For example:

SPEND THIS SUMMER IN A LIGHTHOUSE

Enjoy the peace and quiet and the wide open sea.
Swim, fish and do all the things you never usually
have time to do. At night, you can relax under the
clear sky and watch the stars. Nothing will disturb you.

COME TO THE SAHARA DESERT...
VISIT THE AMAZON JUNGLE...
THIS YEAR TAKE A TRIP TO THE ANTARCTIC...

Can you think of any other unusual places to go on holiday? With your
neighbour, see if you can write a poster for one of them.

3   What makes a good holiday for you?
Think about it for a few minutes
and, by yourself, make some notes,
like this:

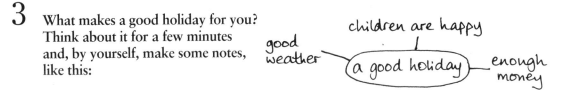

When you have finished, discuss your ideas with the rest of the class. Add more
points to your notes, if you wish.

Now choose the four most important points for you and put them in order.
Use those points to write a paragraph about your ideas. After each point, say
why it is important for you or give some more information. For example:

The most important thing for me is that the children are
happy. If they are happy, everybody is happy.

Here are some ways of introducing each point:

The most important thing for me is . . .
Next, ... is also important for me.   In addition, . . .
Another point is . . .   Finally, . . .

While you are writing, look at what other students have done and see if you
can improve what you have written.

When you have finished, look at the example in the *Answer key* and compare it
with your own paragraph.

9 | A learning workshop

1 Which are the most useful phrases when you are learning English? In pairs, make a 'phrasebook'. Write down some of the things you would say in these situations.

1 You do not understand a word in your book.
2 You want to know if you used the right word.
3 Somebody said something but you did not hear.
4 You have completed an exercise.
5 You do not know how to write a word.
6 Somebody is speaking too quickly.
7 The teacher is not talking about the page you are looking at.
8 You do not know how to say a word in English.
9 You want to compare your work with your neighbour's.
10 You did not come to the last lesson.

Can you think of any other useful classroom phrases? Add them to your list.

When you are ready, compare your phrasebook with other students in your class.

2 Which is the most important for you: reading, writing, speaking or listening? Which are you best at? Copy the chart below and put a number 1–4 to show the order for you. Then, note down the things you want or need to do in English. Like this:

	How important?	How good am I?	I need/want to . . .
Reading	1	3	– read letters at work – read English newspapers
Writing	2	1	
Speaking	4	4	– ask for things in shops and hotels on holiday
Listening	3	2	

When you are ready, compare your chart with other students in your class.

3 Look back at your chart from Exercise 2. In a small group, try to make a list of ways you can improve your English. Like this:

<u>Listening</u> – listen to English and American radio stations
  – buy 'book and cassette' stories
  – rent English or American videos and cover the subtitles

Share your ideas with the rest of the class.

4 You can also improve your English by making your own exercises. There are some examples below. Choose one and try to do it and then make another exercise like it for other people in your class to do. Remember to write the answers on the back of your paper.*

A

Join the right halves of words to the right clue.

umbr ains   in front of the window
sal   tiful   costs a lot
expe ycle   somewhere to grow flowers
beau ella   money from work
gar   ling   it has two wheels
cei   nsive   the top of the room
curt ary   useful if it rains
bic   den   very attractive

Look back at your coursebook and make your own exercise using new words you have recently learnt.

B

Can you put the words in each sentence in the right order and then put the sentences in the right order?

Well, go down this you road straight and turn left   .   can't You it miss   .
Street me, do Excuse you where Green is know   ?
all at Not   .
thank Oh, you   .   (*rather surprised*)
don't No, I sorry, I'm   .

Find a short passage or dialogue in your coursebook. Mix up the words in each sentence and then mix up the sentences.

---

* There are some more examples of practice exercises that you can use in *Writing 1*, Unit 6.

C

Can you find the answers to these questions in the passage below?

1 Where was Herbert Smith going?
2 What happened to the radio?
3 Why did he stop the car?
4 Why did he stand still?
5 Are the following sentences true, false or don't we know?
    – It was raining.
    – Mr Smith's torch did not work.
    – It was a man who said his name.
    – Mr Smith was frightened.

It was three o'clock on a January morning and Herbert Smith was on his way back home from a meeting in London. As he drove along the road, he could see the stars shining brightly against the clear black sky. He turned on the radio and sang as he drove. Things had gone well for him that day.

Suddenly, the radio went off. He turned the switch on and off a few times but nothing happened. It was dead, completely dead. Strange, he thought. Never mind, I'll be home soon. He drove for a mile or two and then as he turned a corner, his lights suddenly went out. Quickly, he stopped the car and took a torch out of the pocket in the door. He turned it on and got out of the car. The moon shone brightly above him as he opened the bonnet and looked into the engine. Perhaps it's a bad contact, he thought, and shone the light around the battery. It was just then, as he was looking at the battery, that he began to feel that someone was standing behind him. He stood still, not sure what to do. Then he felt it, a tap on his shoulder. 'Mr Smith', a voice said, 'Mr Herbert Smith'.

Find a short text in your coursebook and write some questions about it. (Remember to say which page the text is on.)

10 | Lifetimes

1   If you apply for a job, you often need to say what you have done in life. Here are the CVs of four people who have applied for a job to look after children in a kindergarten. Who would you employ? Discuss it with the rest of the class.

CURRICULUM VITAE

Name: Henry Wilson

Date of birth: 16 July 1954

Place of birth: Ipplepen, England

1959-65	Ipplepen Primary School
1965-72	Ipplepen Secondary School
1973-74	Travelling in India
1974-79	Living in a commune in Sweden
1979	Unemployed in England
1980-83	Shop assistant, Computers Ltd
1983-87	B.A. degree in Computer Science, University of London
1987	Computer Programmer, National Bank
1988-91	Travelling in Australia
1992-	Unemployed

Interests

Reading, playing the guitar, playing games and painting

Curriculum Vitae

Name: Susan Smith

Date of birth: 13 February 1949

Place of birth: Worcester, England

1954-59	Ryelands Primary School, Worcester
1959-64	St Rose Secondary School
1964-68	Typist, Norton Plastics Ltd
1969-86	Secretary, Kingswood Bank
1986-	At home, looking after my children

Interests

Walking, reading and travelling

```
        Curriculum Vitae

Name: Arthur Newman
Date of birth: 12 August 1924
Place of birth: Dayton, Ohio, USA

1929-39    Wilfred Randal School, Dayton, Ohio
1939-48    Hunter Biscuit Factory, factory worker
1948-51    Hunter Biscuit Factory, supervisor
1951-60    Hunter Biscuit Factory, manager
1960       I left Hunter Biscuits to start my own business
1962       I employed 20 people at my factory
1968       I employed 60 people at my factory
1973       I employed 200 people at my factory
1979       I bought Hunter Biscuits and formed a new
           company, Hunter-Newman Cakes Ltd
1989       I sold Hunter-Newman Cakes Ltd; I am now retired


Interests
Singing, watching TV and playing football
```

```
          CURRICULUM VITAE
Name: Nicki Chapman
Date of birth: 23 March 1959
Place of birth: Manama, Bahrain

1970-77    Westfield Comprehensive School, Lancaster
1977-80    B.A. in Art and Design, University of Bristol
1980-81    Trainee Manager, Fine Foods Supermarkets Ltd
1981-83    Singer in "The String Band" folk music group; recorded 2 LPs
           and toured Europe and Japan
1984-85    Unemployed
1986-87    Course in Sculpture, Stafford College of Art
1988-91    Tourist guide in Athens


Interests
Music, sculpture and painting
```

2 Look at the CVs in Exercise 1 again and write a CV about yourself.

When you have finished, pass your CVs around. Imagine that everybody in
your class wants to change jobs. What jobs do you think would be good for
each person? Note down your ideas and then compare them with what the
person who wrote the CV thinks.

3   Life always has its ups and downs. Draw a graph to show how you see life and
     add some notes about the main events in life. You can draw a graph about life
     in general:

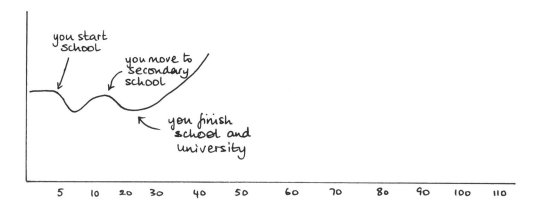

Or, if you prefer, about how you see your own life:

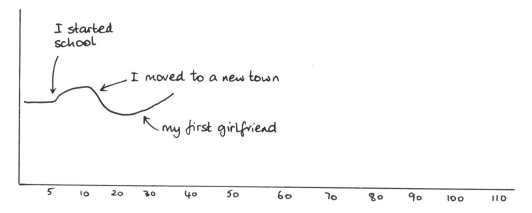

When you are ready, compare your graph with other students' graphs. Do you
all see life in the same way?

4 Look at your graph again. Which is the best time in life? When you are a child? A teenager? An adult? At work? At school? Retired? Discuss it with the rest of the class.

Write a short paragraph about your ideas. If you prefer, make some notes first to help you write. For example:

As a teenager
- lots of friends
- life is exciting
- things to do
- you feel active

I think that the best time in life is when you are a teenager. You usually have lots of friends and life is very exciting. There are lots of new things to do and see and you feel very active.

While you are writing, compare with what other students in your class have written. See if there are any ways you can improve what you have written.

11 | Write soon

1   When do people send greetings cards? What messages do they choose? Match the messages below with the occasions. Two occasions are missing. What do you think they are? (Some messages can be used more than once.)

1 Congratulations	a) any time
2 Best wishes	b) someone has died
3 Happy . . .	c) ....
4 Good luck	d) a birthday / anniversary / new year / Christmas
5 Season's greetings	e) Christmas / Easter
6 Bon voyage	f) someone has got a new job
7 Get well soon	g) someone is going to take an exam
8 With sympathy	h) someone has passed an exam
	i) someone is getting married
	j) ....

2   Often, when people send a card they add a short message. Here are some messages. What do you think it says on the front of the card?

a)

We hope you have a wonderful time in Tahiti. Send us a postcard when you arrive. We'll look forward to seeing you when you come back next June.

Pat and John

b)

I hope the exams are not too difficult. I'm sure they will go well for you.
Love,
Sue

We are all thinking about you at the office and we hope that you can come back to work soon.

Steve
Isabel   *Nadia*
Peter   *Hans*

c)

Now choose one or two of the situations below. First write down what the front of the card would say and then write a short message to put inside it.

1 Next week is your friend's birthday. She is living in Nigeria at the moment but she is coming home for a visit next month.

2 You have just come back from a holiday in England. You want to send a card to the family you stayed with.

3 A friend helped you a lot recently when you were ill. You want to send him/her a small present.

4 A friend has just had a baby. She is still in hospital at the moment. You will visit her at home when she comes out.

5 A friend is going to take his driving test next week. It is his sixth time.

3 Sometimes you can send a short letter to give some news. John Banton has just moved house and he wants to tell his friends his new address. His letter is on page 36, but some parts are missing. What do you think he wrote? Write down your ideas and then compare with your neighbour.

56, Strathdene Rd
Birmingham
BR9 5HD
Tel. 021-472-8911

26th November

Dear Bob,

I'm sorry I haven't written for such a long time. How are you? We ...

We have just moved house (see our new address above). It's ...

Sarah has just started school. She's ...

Otherwise, life is just the same. I get up, I go to work, I eat, I sleep, I get up. Very exciting!

Anyway, write soon and ...

Best wishes,

John

4   Imagine that you have not seen the other students in your class for a long time. Write a letter to one of them. Tell him/her how you are and give some news about yourself. (You can invent something if you like. For example: you are going to change jobs, you are getting married, you have won £10,000 or you are going on a long trip.)

Dear Jan,

How are you? I haven't seen you for such a long time. ...

Read the letter that you receive and send a suitable 'greetings card' to the person you get the letter from. (Fold a piece of paper in half.) Write a short message inside. Thank him/her for the letter and say how you are and what you are doing.

Good luck

with your English exam.
Thanks for the letter. I
was sorry to hear that
you were ill.

Best wishes,
Louise

12 | What's it for?

1 Here are some modern inventions. What is each one for? With your neighbour, note down your answers and then try to label the parts of each picture. Use a dictionary to help you. For example:

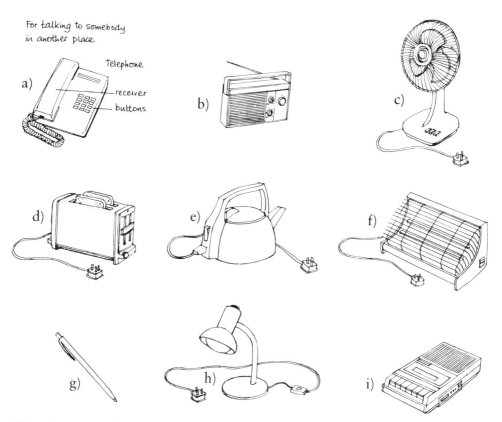

How do you use the things above? Write a sentence or two about each one. Like this:

a) If you want to talk to somebody in another place, lift the receiver and press the buttons for the number you want.

2

Here is another invention, but this is more unusual. What do you think it is for? Choose definition A, B or C.

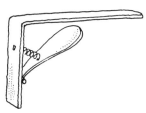

A This is for breaking nuts. You put the nut in the centre, pull back the lever and let go.

B This is a musical instrument. You open and close it to make it click.

C This is for holding a table cloth on to a table. You open it and put it on the edge of the table.

Now divide into groups, Group A and Group B. Each group should look at their pictures below and try to make up three possible uses for each thing. Group A should see page 68 and Group B should see page 77 for help. (Don't look at the other group's page!)

When you're ready, read out, in any order, the three uses for each item. The other group has to guess which one is the real use.

Pictures for Group A:

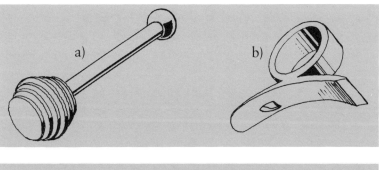

Pictures for Group B:

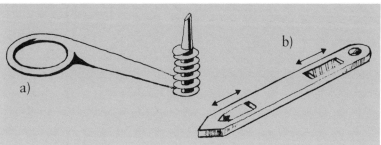

3

Even ordinary things can sound unusual. What is this?

A thingummy is made of metal, glass and leather. People wear them on their arms. Sometimes they wear them because they think they look nice, but usually they wear them because they need them. They need to know what time it is.

In pairs, think of two or three ordinary things. Write a description of each one but say 'thingummy' instead of its name. You can write about anything you like: something in the room, something at home, something at work, something in the street, an animal, a plant – anything. You can say what it is made of, what shape it has and what people do with it.

When you are ready, pass your papers round. Can you guess what the other people have written about?

13 | Puzzle time

This unit has three exercises. Work with a partner and start on any exercise you like. When you have finished an exercise, ask if anyone has a puzzle for you to do before you move on to another exercise.

1 This is a simple word puzzle. How many words can you make? You must follow the straight lines. Use your dictionary to help you.

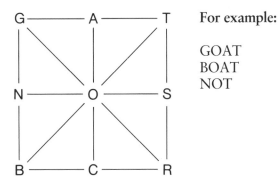

For example:

GOAT
BOAT
NOT

Now make a puzzle for another pair of students to do. This is how:

On the first line, write: consonant – vowel – consonant
On the second line, write: consonant – vowel – consonant
On the third line, write: consonant – consonant – consonant
The consonants that you can use are:
  B C D F G H K L M N P R S T
The vowels that you can use are:
  A E I O U
Don't use:
  J Q V W X Y Z

See how many words *you* can make and write your list of words on the back of the paper.

2 Can you do crosswords? Here is an easy one.

Clues

Across

2 To fall into pieces. (5)
4 A glass container. (6)
6 I'm not hungry. I ..... a lot for breakfast. (3)
8 There are three ways to write it: two, too and ..... . (2)
9 They catch criminals. (6)
12 A very large animal. (8)
16 The sun rises in the ..... and sets in the west. (4)
18 I'll come ..... soon as possible. (2)
19 Your age on your first birthday. (3)
20 By yourself. (4)

Down

1 Somewhere to wait for a bus. (4)
2 Infinitive from 'was'. (2)
3 I'm so hungry I could ..... a horse. (3)
4 Paul McCartney was one of these. (6)

5 This is useful if you want to see at night. (4)
7 A fast plane. (3)
10 This: _____ .(4)
11 Please give it to ..... . (2)
13 Norway has ..... oil than Saudi Arabia. (4)
14 Somewhere to swim. (4)
15 At the end of a dog. (4)
17 If you stay in the sun, you can get one. (3)

Now make a crossword for another pair of students to do. This is how you can do it:

1 First, draw a square like the one above (10 x 10). Write in some words across and down. Put ■ in the squares that you do not need. (Make sure you spell the words correctly!)
2 Number the start of each word.
3 On another piece of paper, write a clue for each word. (You can write a definition or a sentence with the word missing.)
4 When you have written all the clues, copy your square underneath – without the letters!

3

Read the letter below and then look at the picture. How many things can you find that are wrong in the picture?

27th February

Dear Steve,

How are you? I haven't heard from you for a long time. We're all fine.

I'm sitting here by the fire, writing a letter to you. Jim's here as well. He's ironing some shirts to wear to work next week. Sam and Elizabeth are in bed, thank goodness! It was Sam's birthday today (he's 10 now). He and Elizabeth took the dog out for a walk today but unfortunately the dog didn't come back. I'm not going to work tomorrow (Sunday) so perhaps I can go and look for him. I hope he's OK.

Grandfather is staying with us at the moment. He's fast asleep in the armchair, snoring loudly. He fell down yesterday and broke his foot. He's got it in plaster.

Anyway, I have to go now. I want to see the news at ten o'clock and it's going to start in five minutes.

Write and tell us how you are. Why don't you come and visit us soon?

Love
Margaret

Now look at the picture below and write a letter from Margaret to another friend, Helen. Write some things in the letter that are different from the picture, which other students have to find. For example, you can write about:

– the weather
– the day and time
– where she is
– who is there
– what everybody is doing
– what has happened
– what they are going to do

Dear Helen,

How are you? I haven't heard from you for a long time. We're all fine.

I'm sitting here ...

14 | Describing people

1 Look at the pictures below and try to match each one to the correct description. Each person was famous in their own country and abroad. Do you know his/her name? When you are ready, compare your answers with your neighbour and then look in the *Answer key*.

1 In this picture, he was quite old. He had thick white hair and a bushy moustache. His face was very wrinkled and he had a very high forehead. His eyebrows were quite dark. He looked a very kind, soft and artistic person.

2 In this picture, he was in his early forties. He had a squarish face with a small mouth and very even, white teeth. His hair was short and dark. He looked a very strong, determined person.

3 In this picture, she was in her sixties. Her hair was going grey. She had dark eyes, dark eyebrows and a large nose. She looked a very serious, honest person.

4 She was probably in her twenties when they took this picture. Her hair was short and curly and she looked very beautiful. She had bright, wide eyes and soft, smooth skin. She looked a very calm, sophisticated person.

5 It is hard to say how old she was when they took this picture. She had a roundish face with a double chin, lots of very curly black hair, bright, smiling eyes and a very friendly smile. She looked a very cheerful, pleasant person.

6 He had a very solid, squarish face with large ears, a double chin, a long nose and staring eyes. His head was almost completely bald and he had a very serious, stern look on his face. He looked a very stern, unfriendly person.

a)

b)

c)

d)

e)

f)

Now read through the descriptions again and make a list of the words you can use to describe a person's face, eyes, mouth, nose, hair and general impression. Like this:

<u>face</u>	<u>eyes</u>	<u>mouth</u>	<u>nose</u>	<u>hair</u>	<u>general impression</u>
roundish	small	wide	long	long	proud
			pointed	curly	

With the rest of the class, see what other words you can add to each column.

2 There are some more photographs of people below. Using your list of words, write a description of two or three. When you have finished, ask your neighbour to see if he/she can identify them. Like this:

The person has a roundish face and short blond hair. He has rather large eyes and a small nose. His skin looks very soft. He looks like a very pleasant, peaceful person.

Compare your descriptions with those of other students who wrote about the same photographs.

3 Sometimes, you need to give a lot more information about people – yourself, for example. Imagine that you have just written a book – a novel, a travel guide, a cook book or something like that. What would it say inside the cover? Think for a few moments and make some notes. Like this:

- born in Kenya
- married with 2 children
- worked as: cook, teacher, writer
- interests: cycling and walking
- lives in Paris, works at home

Now, using your notes, write a paragraph about yourself. For example:

The author was born in Mombasa, Kenya and is married with two small children, aged 3 and 7. She has worked as a cook, a teacher and now as a writer. Her main interests in addition to cooking are cycling and walking. At the moment she lives in Paris where she works at home.

When you are ready, pass your paragraphs around the class. See if you can guess who 'the author' is of each paragraph.

4 Think back to your childhood. Try to remember a friend you once had. Note down your answers to these questions:

How old were you?
What was his/her name?
What did he/she look like?
What did you use to do together?
Where did he/she live?
Do you know where he/she is now?
What other things can you remember about him/her?

>>>→

Now write a paragraph about your friend. This, for example, is about a child-hood friend that I used to have:

When I was about five or six years old I used to have a friend called Helen Arthur. She was very tall and thin with short brown hair, a roundish face and a small nose. I remember we used to play in the street and in her garden. She lived in the house next to mine. She had a brother called Tim, who was about five years older than her. I don't know where Helen is now or what she is doing. The last time I saw her was about 25 years ago, just before I started secondary school.

When you have finished, exchange papers with some other students in the class and discuss your paragraph with them. Can they suggest any ways to improve what you have written?

Ask a few students to read out what they have written. Does anybody still have the same friend now that they had when they were a child?

15 | Looking at writing

1 Which works best for you – 'accurate' writing or 'fluent' writing? Try an experiment. First do section A and then section B.

A
You have 15 minutes. Choose one of the topics in the box at the bottom of the page (or any other topic) and first make some notes. Like this:

My job
- travel agent
- in an office
- I like it
- long day, low salary
- travel sometimes
- meet new people

Then think about what you will write. Put your notes in order.

My job
1 - travel agent
2 - in an office
5 - I like it
4 - long day, low salary
3 - travel sometimes
6 - meet new people

Finally, join your points together as you write. Try NOT to make any mistakes. Only write what you know is correct.

I work as a travel agent. I usually work in a large office although sometimes I have to travel around the country to visit people. My days are very long and my salary is not very good but I like my job because I meet lots of new people.

When you have finished, put your paper to one side.

> **Topics:**
> my dream house   my job   space   school   food   holidays
> clothes   travel   my family   my country   why I want to learn English

B
Now choose another topic. You have 10 minutes to write as much as you can. Just write down what comes into your head. Don't worry about mistakes. Like this:

I come from a large family. 5 boys and 3 girls.

I'm the youngest. They are in Bangkok – I'm here.

In the summer, I want to go home to see my family.

My father is an old man. 85. My mother visited me

here last year. She liked it very much.

When you have finished, you can have another five minutes but, this time, do not write anything new. Just try to correct and change what you have written. Like this:

There are eight of us,
five three
I come from a large family, 5 boys and 3 girls, and
am all live but live
I'm the youngest. They are in Bangkok, I'm here.
Next
In the summer, I want to go home to see my family.
Last year
My father is an old man. 85. My mother visited me
m
here. last year She liked it very much. My father
didn't come because he was too old to travel. He
is now 85.

Which worked best for you? Compare what you wrote in A and B. Show your writing to your neighbour. Which worked best for him/her? Find out what other people in your class think.

2

Here are some common mistakes that people make when they are learning English. Can you match the type of mistake to each example?

My brother lives in London.

Yesterday, I go to the cinema.

How is you?

Tokyo is a very large citee.

I want speak to Mr Brown, please.

I don't know what is his name.

word order
spelling
word missing
wrong tense
wrong form
punctuation

What are *your* common mistakes? Look back at some of the things you have written in English and make a list of the mistakes you usually make. Compare your list with your neighbour's. You can use your list to check anything you write in the future.

Many people use a mnemonic to help them remember what to check. Here, for example, is one student's mnemonic:

PATTIBS

1 Punctuation
2 Articles (a/an/the)
3 There is/are
4 Tenses (especially past tense and present perfect)
5 -ing (e.g. He is smoking.)
6 Be (am/is/are/was/were)
7 Spelling

Try to make a mnemonic of your common mistakes to help you remember. Use it to check your work every time you write something.

16 | The Earth is . . .

1 The Earth is a planet with a lot of variety: everything from very wet, cold places to very hot, dry places, and from very crowded places to very empty places. How do you see the different parts of the world? Think about each of the six continents and make some notes about each one. Like this:

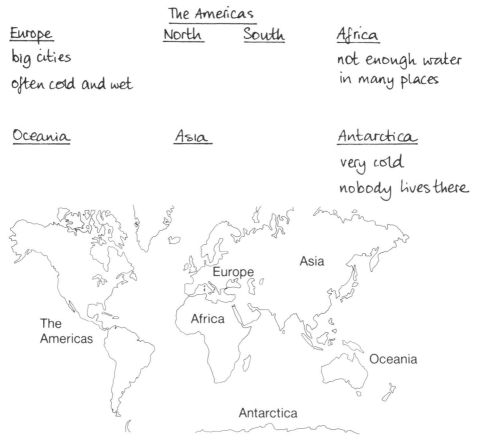

The Americas

Europe   North   South   Africa
big cities   not enough water
often cold and wet   in many places

Oceania   Asia   Antarctica
                                    very cold
                                    nobody lives there

(If you prefer, think about a particular country in each continent.)

When you have finished, compare with what other people in your class noted down. Which part of the world do you think is most interesting or do you most like? Discuss your ideas with the rest of the class.

2 Do you like living where you live now or would you like to live in another part of the world? Why? Look back on your notes from Exercise 1 and write a short paragraph about your ideas. Like this:

I would like to live in Mexico or somewhere in South

America. Although there are a lot of problems there,

I think the people are very friendly. There are also

a lot of interesting plants, animals and places. I

think that life is quite difficult there but it is a lot

more exciting. The sun shines a lot and that would

give me energy.

When you are ready, give your paper to another student to read. Read the paragraph that you receive and add some questions that you would like to know more about. For example:

What problems are there?
What interesting places are there in Mexico?

When you get your paper back, see if you can put the answers to some of the questions into your paragraph. Like this:

I would like to live in Mexico or somewhere in South
                                    such as high inflation
America. Although there are a lot of problems there,

I think the people are very friendly. There are also
                    for example, I would like to visit the Mayan pyramids
a lot of interesting plants, animals and places. I

think that life is quite difficult there but it is a lot

more exciting. The sun shines a lot and that would

give me energy.

3 The Earth is now 18,000 million years old. It has had a lot of good times and a lot of bad times. What things do you think the Earth feels happy about? What things does it feel bad about? If you could give the Earth a present, what would it be? Discuss this with the rest of the class.

Imagine the Earth is talking to the Moon. What do they say to each other? Write their conversation, like this:

Write on a piece of paper:

Hello, Earth. How are you?

and then pass the paper to the person on your left. On the paper you receive, write your answer as the Earth and then pass it back. Now write your next reply as the Moon on the paper you receive and pass it back. Continue like this as Moon then Earth, Moon then Earth for 10 minutes or so.

When you have finished, read through your conversation and see if you want to make any corrections. Then exchange papers with some other pairs. Read out some conversations to the rest of the class.

4 The Earth is . . . A chain poem
The Earth is more than a planet. Work in a small group and write a poem about what you think and feel about the Earth. Like this:

Take a piece of paper and write 'The Earth is' and then finish the sentence as you want. Fold over the top of the paper and pass it on to the person next to you. Write another 'The Earth is' sentence. Fold the paper and pass it on. Do this four more times.

When you have finished, read out your poems to your group. Then, in your group, choose the six best sentences to make a new 'The Earth is' poem. Read out your poem to the class.

17 | Body talk

🔑

1 In most cultures, people communicate with gestures as well as words. Do the gestures below mean anything in your culture? Write down what they mean to you – if anything. For example:

a) This means 'everything is fine' or 'no problem'.

When you have finished, exchange papers with another student in your class. Compare what you have both written.

a)   b)   c)   d)   e)   f)   g)   h)   i)   j)   k)

What other gestures do you use in your culture? Think for a few minutes and note down what they mean and then show the rest of the class.

2

Our clothes and our actions also communicate something. What are these people 'saying'? Discuss them with your neighbour and write a few sentences about each one. For example:

a)

'I am respectable and reliable and you can trust me with your business. I think about my work seriously and I always try to do my best. I am quite a friendly person, so don't be afraid to ask me any questions. I will try to help if I can.'

b)

c)

d)

e)

Find out what other students in your class thought.

3 Our faces, eyes and expressions also say a lot, often about our life in general. Look at the photographs below. What can you see in each face? Think carefully and write a few sentences about your impressions of four of them. For example:

Photo a)

I think this person is about forty to forty-five years old. He could be an artist or a potter or something like that. He looks very serious and I expect he is a rather quiet person. He doesn't look very friendly and he probably doesn't have many friends. On the other hand, it is possible that he has a problem at the moment and that usually he is much happier.

When you have finished, find out what others in the class wrote about each of the photographs. Are your general impressions similar?

4 Now look back at the two photographs in Exercise 3 that you did not write about. Choose one of them and imagine that you are that person. Think about the impressions that other people in your class had about that person and note down your answers to these questions:

Where are you?
Why do you have that expression on your face right now?
What has just happened?
What are you going to do next?
What are you thinking about right now?

Now, using your notes, write a paragraph about your thoughts as that person. Who, for example, do you think is thinking this:

I hope they don't notice. What am I going to say? It wasn't my fault that the window broke. I didn't mean to do it. We were only playing a game and the ball hit it. Anyway, Sita told me to kick it as hard as I could. It's her fault. I could say I don't know anything about it. Would they believe me? Probably not. They never believe me. If I start crying now they will know I did it. I mustn't cry. Oh no, they're calling me inside. I know I'm going to cry.

(If you prefer, write down your imaginary thoughts in your own language first. This will help you get ideas. Write something simple and then try to write more or less the same thing in English.)

While you are writing in English, compare with your neighbour. Help each other with spellings, phrasing, etc. Can you see any ways to improve what you have each written?

When you have finished, pass your papers around the class. Read the paper that you receive. Which photograph do you think it is about?

18 | Writing for yourself

*Writing is often a good way to think about and remember things. If you try to
do this in English, you can learn words that are useful for you at the same time.
In this unit you can see some ways of writing for yourself.*

1 We often use writing to help us plan what we have to do. For example:

Shopping lists

> Things to buy
>
> 3kg sugar
> 2 litres of milk
> a lettuce
> a cucumber

Reminders to do something

> Friday
> – ring the doctor's
> – post the parcel to Jan
> – buy the traveller's cheques
> – collect the tickets
> – buy a present to take

Lists of things to take somewhere

> To take
> passport   camera + films
> tickets   book
> money
> credit card
> pens, paper and envelopes
> radio
> shaver

Notes for a letter, meeting or
telephone call

> Letter applying for a job
>
> 4 – children now at school
> 2 – I worked for Brook's Bank until 1988
> 3 – after that, at home looking after
>   the children
> 1 – I saw the advertisement in the Daily
>   Advertiser
> 5 – they can ring Mrs Lee at Brook's

Plans of things to do

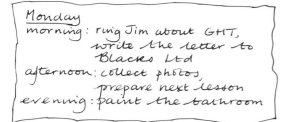

Ideas or word maps

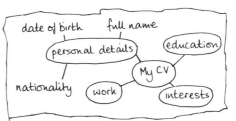

Think of one or two things that you have to do or write in the next few days and choose some of the ways above to help you plan. When you have finished, look at the ways that other students used.

2 How was last week for you? From the list below choose a few adjectives that describe different aspects of the week. (You can add some more adjectives of your own if you wish.)

exciting   boring   happy   fun   interesting
tiring   sad   serious   relaxing   stressful   busy
terrible   romantic   pleasant   normal   frightening

Now write a sentence or two beside each adjective to explain why you chose it. For example:

<u>relaxing</u>   I sat in the garden on Monday morning and wrote some letters.

<u>frightening</u> Daniel fell over on Sunday and hit his head. We had to take him to the hospital. He's OK now.

If you like, give your list to another student to read. Compare your week with his/hers.

3 Think about a particular day last week and write a diary for that day. Choose one of the following to help you think about what to write. You can use your dictionary to help you.

1 What did you do that day? What happened? For example:

I went to the library and found a very interesting book. It was so interesting that I sat in the library until 7.30 and missed my bus. I had to walk home and it was raining. When I arrived home, I was wet and hungry. I was in a very bad temper.

2 Think about three people that you met that day. What did they have on? What were they doing? How were they?

I met Nadeem at the bus stop in the morning. He was wearing his blue shirt and striped trousers. He said he was going shopping but he seemed a bit tired. I think he may be ill. I also met ...

3 What were the positive things about the day? What were the negative things?

<u>Positive things</u>

A good day at work. I did a lot and everybody was very happy in the office. The children played together very well. Rachel painted a beautiful picture. We put it on the wall.

<u>Negative things</u>

Another late night! I didn't write the letter to Pat. It's a very difficult letter and I don't know what to say.

If you would like to, read or show your diary entry to other students in the class. Try to keep a diary in English for a few days or weeks.

4 You can also use writing to help you think about how things are for you generally at the moment. For example:

Life is generally quite good at the moment. I am playing a lot of tennis and I feel very fit. Work is a little bit boring but the people there are friendly. Perhaps I will try to change my job soon. I would like to work nearer to my home because, at the moment, I have to travel almost three hours every day. I enjoy my English lessons but I think it is quite a difficult language to learn. Perhaps I am getting old!

If you find it difficult to write in English, one idea is to write in your language first. This will help you organise your ideas. Write something simple and, while you are writing, think about what you can say in English. Then try to write more or less the same thing in English.

19 | Look after yourself

1 Below are some common injuries and complaints. Imagine that you have to write a leaflet on 'First Aid at Home'. What advice would you put for each one? Work with a partner and write down your ideas. You can use your dictionary to help you. Like this:

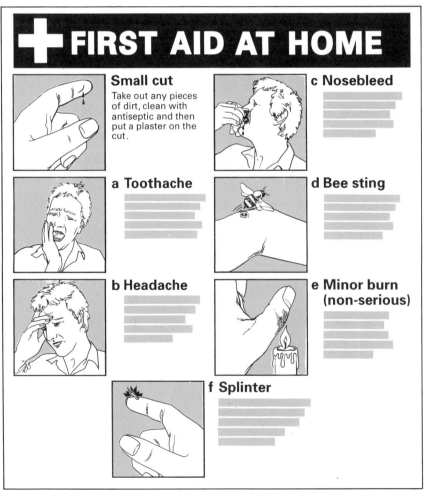

FIRST AID AT HOME

Small cut
Take out any pieces of dirt, clean with antiseptic and then put a plaster on the cut.

c Nosebleed

a Toothache

d Bee sting

b Headache

e Minor burn (non-serious)

f Splinter

When you have finished, compare with what other students have written. Do you all agree on the best thing to do in each case?

2 There are many 'natural' ways to cure and heal. Do you know any? What things would you put in a 'natural' first aid kit? In a small group, make a list of some items and what you can do with them. For example:

A Natural First Aid Kit: Contents

A piece of beef.   You can use this to put on black eyes.

Here, for example, is one Natural First Aid Kit. Do you know what each thing is for?

3 Our health is more than just cuts, stings and colds. What things affect our health generally? Discuss this with the rest of the class and note down the points that people make. For example:

Things that affect your health
- how many hours you sleep each night
- your job (do you sit down all day?)
- how much exercise you do

Now, in a small group, choose ten of the points and make a questionnaire. Write three or four possible answers for each question. Like this:

1 How many hours do you sleep each night?
   a) over 8 hours
   b) 5–8 hours
   c) less than 5 hours

2 At work, do you sit down:
   a) all the time?
   b) about half the time?
   c) less than half the time?
   d) almost never?

Next, write a key for the questions. Give a score to each answer in order of how healthy you think each point is.

Question 1: a = 3, b = 4, c = 2
Question 2: a = 1, b = 2, c = 4, d = 3

Then write a key for the total score. For example:

31–40: You have a very healthy life.
21–30: You need to change the way you live soon.

When you have finished, exchange questionnaires with another group and answer their questions. Do you agree with what their questionnaire says about the way you live?

20 | The real you

1 If you meet an 11 or 12 year-old child, what questions might you ask him/her? Think for a few moments and write down as many questions as you can think of.

> What's your name?
> Where do you live?
> What are your favourite games?

What questions did other students in your class think of?

Now imagine that you are walking along a beach and you can see a child playing in the sand. As you get closer, you see that it is your neighbour when he/she was much younger. Talk to him/her and ask some of your questions. Your neighbour must answer as if he/she were 11 or 12 years old again.

What did you find out? Write a few sentences about the 'child' you spoke to.

> The child I spoke to lives in a large, old house near
> Milan. She has three sisters and two brothers. She
> says that she is the youngest and cleverest in her
> family. She likes playing tennis and making models.
> She says she wants to be a doctor when she gets
> older...

When you're ready, pass your papers around. Can you guess who each 'child' is?

2 Imagine that you are going for a walk in the woods. On the way, you find
some things and you have to decide what you will do with them. Read through
sections 1 to 7 below and discuss with the other people in your class what you
could write for each one.

1 You are walking in a wood. What is it like? Is it light or dark? Is the sun
shining? What can you see, hear or smell? How do you feel?

I'm walking through a wood. It's ... and I can... I feel ...

2 You are walking along a path. What is it like? Is it straight? Is it stony? Is it
easy to see?

The path that I'm walking on is ...

3 On the ground in front of you, you find a key. What is it like? Is it clean or
rusty? How big is it? What do you do with it?

In front of me, on the ground, I find a key. It's ... and I ...

4 You walk on for some time and then you come to some water. What is it? a
river? a lake? How is it? clean? dirty? Is it moving? Is it deep? What do you
do?

*After a while, I come to some water. It's ... and the water
is ..., I ...*

5 A little while later, you come to a house. You walk round the house and
look inside. What do you see? What does the house look like? Is the house in
good condition or in ruins? What do you do?

Sometime later, I come to a house. It's ... and ... I ...

6 Back on the path, you come to a wall in front of you. What is it like? Is it in
good condition? How high is it? You manage to look over the wall. What
do you see on the other side?

*I get back on to the path but then I come to a wall. The
wall is ... On the other side of it, I can see ...*

7 The wall is across your path, in front of you. What do you do next?

The wall is across my path, so I ...

Now, by yourself, copy the sentences that start each section and continue them to describe *your* walk in the woods. Add as much detail as you like. As you finish each part, move on to the next.

When you have finished, look in the *Answer key* to find out what it all means! If you like, compare your 'walk in the woods' with your neighbour's. Tell the rest of the class some of the things you found out about yourself.

Unit 12   What's it for?

2   Notes for Group A

In your group, write three possible uses for each of the two things in your pictures. One of the uses must be the correct one.

a) The correct use:

Here are some other possible uses, but you can invent other ones:

b) The correct use:

Here are some other possible uses, but you can invent other ones:

Answer key

Unit 1 The good life

3   The house is in Yucatan, in the south of Mexico on the Caribbean sea.

Unit 2 Time to spare

4   *Poem 1*: The person was lying on a beach, on holiday with his children. He was very happy to be there.
Poem 2: The person was waiting at a railway station for a train, on her way to work. She felt tired and under pressure. She felt that she had no time for herself.
Poem 3: The person was at home waiting for his girlfriend to ring. He was worried about her and felt nervous.

Unit 3 A photo album

4

Unit 4 Are you free?

1   a) – f);   c) – d);   e) – b)

Invitation (c) and reply (d) are the most formal. There are no short forms (e.g. I'm, I'll, Thanks) and the words are very formal (e.g. 'request the pleasure of the company of . . . ', 'yours sincerely').

Unit 5   Food, glorious food

1   The ingredients for each dish may vary, but they generally include the following:

Spain, paella: rice, saffron, onions, seafood, chicken   (g)
Mexico, tacos: maize flour (for the tortillas), meat, beans, lettuce, cheese, chilli
   sauce   (c)
Italy, spaghetti bolognese: pasta, minced meat, tomatoes, onions, herbs, garlic,
   parmesan cheese   (f)
India, curry: meat, spices, rice   (a)
England, roast beef and Yorkshire pudding: beef, Yorkshire pudding (flour, milk,
   egg, oil)   (d)
Switzerland, fondue: cheese, Kirsch, white wine, garlic, cornflour   (e)
Germany, sausage and sauerkraut; sausage and pickled cabbage   (b)

3

good	bad	good or bad
delicious	burnt	cold
fresh	greasy	soft
tasty	stale	sweet
tender	overcooked	warm
	tough	salty
	undercooked	raw
		hard
		hot

Unit 6   For sale

2   **Possible answer:**
For sale. 1988 Renault 5. Terrible condition, lots of rust, very badly damaged,
one flat tyre, seats ripped, very high mileage, very dirty.

Unit 7   Please read carefully

1   a) Please do not touch. / Careful! / Please ask the assistant for help.
    b) Please take one. / Please take a leaflet.
    c) Keep away from children. / Keep in a safe place away from children.
    d) Break the glass. / In case of fire, break the glass.
    e) Fragile. / Handle with care.
    f) Please do not walk on the grass. / Keep off the grass. / No dogs.
    g) Quiet please. / No smoking.
    h) Silence.
    i) No jumping. No running. No shouting.

2   **Possible answers:**
    a) It is next to the television, on the left.
    b) It is between the bed and the table.
    c) It is next to the piano, on the right.
    d) It is at the top of the stairs.
    e) It is at the bottom of the stairs.
    f) It is behind the door.
    g) It is in front of the window.
    h) It is in the corner.

Unit 8   Holiday time

3   **Example paragraph:**
The most important thing for me is that the children are happy. If they are happy, everybody is happy. Next, the place has to be interesting. There have to be things to do and see. I don't like just sitting on a beach all day long. The hotel where we stay is also important. It has to be clean and the food has to be good. I don't want to spend all the holiday in bed with stomach problems. Finally, the people have to be friendly. If the people are horrible, it can make the whole holiday horrible.

Unit 9   A learning workshop

1   **Possible answers:**
  1 Could you tell me what this word means, please?
  2 Is this the right word? Can I say this?
  3 I'm sorry, I didn't hear. Could you say that again, please?
  4 I've finished. Can you check this?
  5 How do you spell XXX? How do you write XXX?
  6 Could you speak more slowly, please?
  7 Excuse me, but which page are you on? Which page are you talking about? Which page are you looking at?
  8 How do you say XXX in English? What's XXX in English?
  9 Would you like to exchange? Do you want to look at what I have written?
  10 I'm sorry I wasn't here last lesson. Did you give any papers out? What did you do?

4   A umbrella – useful if it rains
  salary – money from work
  expensive – costs a lot
  beautiful – very attractive
  garden – somewhere to grow flowers
  ceiling – the top of the room
  curtains – in front of the window
  bicycle – it has two wheels

  B Excuse me, do you know where Green Street is?
  No, I'm sorry, I don't.
  Well, you go straight down this road and turn left. You can't miss it.
  Oh, thank you.   (*rather surprised*)
  Not at all.

  C 1 He was going home.
    2 It suddenly went off.
    3 Because the lights had gone out.
    4 Because he could feel that someone was behind him.
    5 False, false, we don't know, we don't know.

Unit 11   Write soon

1   1 f, h, i;   2 a, d, e, i;   3 d, e;   4 f, g;   5 e;   6 someone is going on a trip;   7 someone is ill;   8 b

2   a) Bon voyage;   b) Good luck;   c) Get well soon

3   **Full text of letter:**
Dear Bob
I'm sorry I haven't written for such a long time. How are you? We're all fine.
    We have just moved house (see our new address above). It's bigger than our last house but we still don't have a garden.
    Sarah has just started school. She's enjoying it very much. She has lots of friends and looks forward to going every day.
    Otherwise, life is the same. I get up, I go to work, I eat, I sleep, I get up. Very exciting!
    Anyway, write soon and let us know how you are.
    Best wishes,
    John

Unit 12   What's it for?

1   **Possible answers:**
b) For listening to radio programmes
c) For keeping cool when it is hot
d) For making toast
e) For boiling water
f) For keeping warm when it is cold
g) For writing with
h) For helping you to see when it is dark
i) For playing cassettes

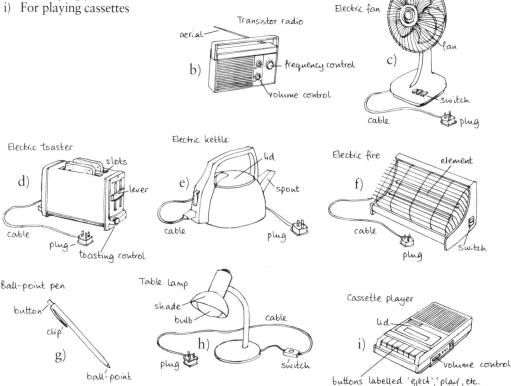

b) If you want to listen to a radio programme, turn on the volume control and tune the radio to the station you want.

c) If you want to keep cool when it is hot, plug the fan in and turn on the switch.

d) If you want to make some toast, plug the toaster in, put some bread into the slots and push down the lever.

e) If you want to boil some water, take off the lid, fill the kettle with water, put the lid back on, plug the kettle in and then press the button.

f) If you want to keep warm when it is cold, plug the fire in and turn on the switch at the side.

g) If you want to write something, push down the button on the top of the pen.

h) If you want to see when it is dark, plug the lamp in and turn on the switch.

i) If you want to play a cassette, press the 'eject' button, put the cassette into the machine, close the lid and press the 'play' button.

2   Definition C is correct.

Possible descriptions:

Group A

a) This is for taking honey out of a pot. You put it into the jar and turn it round.

This is a child's toy. You can spin it on the table.

This is for drawing pictures. You put paint on the end and move it across some paper.

b) This is for peeling an orange. You put the point into the skin and pull it down.

This is for playing the guitar. You hold it in one hand and play the strings with it.

This is for wearing in your hair. You put your hair through the hole.

Group B

a) This is for cutting a cucumber. You put the point into the cucumber and turn the handle.

This is for making a hole in a piece of wood. You put the point into the wood and turn the handle.

This is for cleaning your ears. You put tissue paper on the end and turn it round in your ear.

b) This is for holding a small nail. You put the nail in the end and hold it with the handle. Then you can hit the nail without hitting your thumb.

This is for helping you to take a picture. You look through the hole to see what will be in the picture.

This is for painting with a small brush. You put the brush in the end and hold it with the handle.

3   A watch

Unit 13   Puzzle time

1   **Some words that you can make:**

goat   go   got   no   not   nor   boat   bog   boa   coat
con   cost   rot   rob   sob   son   so   tor   ton

2   **Completed crossword:**

3   **Things wrong in the picture:**
The woman is sitting by the window not by the fire; there is no fire; the dog is
there; Grandfather is not sleeping; the children are not in bed; the clock says it is
10.20, not 9.55; the birthday cards are for Elizabeth, not Sam; the calendar says it
is Tuesday, not Saturday ('tomorrow' is Sunday in the letter).

Unit 14   Describing people

1   1 c Albert Einstein, mathematician and physicist; born Germany, 1879, died
1955.   2 f John F. Kennedy, President of the United States of America; born
1917, died 1963.   3 a Indira Gandhi, first woman Prime Minister of India; born
1917, died 1984.   4 e Greta Garbo, film actress; born Sweden, 1905, died
1990.   5 d Ella Fitzgerald, jazz singer, USA; born 1919.   6 b Winston
Churchill, war-time Prime Minister of Great Britain; born 1874, died 1965.

Unit 15   Looking at writing

2

Example	*Mistake*	*Correct form*
My brother lives in london.	punctuation	London
Yesterday, I go to the cinema.	wrong tense	I went
How is you?	wrong form	How are you?
Tokyo is a very large citee.	spelling	city
I want speak to Mr Brown, please.	word missing	I want to speak
I don't know what is his name.	word order	what his name is

Unit 17   Body talk

1   **Some meanings of the gestures:**

a) In Britain: 'everything is fine', 'no problem'. In Sardinia it is very rude.

b) In Britain: 'crazy'. In some countries (e.g. Holland) it means 'clever'.

c) In Britain: 'very expensive'.

d) In the Arab world: 'no more thank you'.

e) In Britain: 'stop!' In Greece this is very rude.

f) In Britain: 'quieter, please', 'slow down, please'.

g) This means very little in Britain. In Saudi Arabia it means 'stupid'; in Latin America it means 'a beautiful girl'.

h) This means very little in Britain. In Spain, Malta and Italy it is rather rude. In Greece it is a threat.

i) In Britain: 'I can't hear very well. Please speak louder'.

j) In the United States, 'Everything is fine'; in France, 'zero'; in Japan, 'a lot of money'; in Tunisia it is a threat; in Latin America it is very rude.

k) In Britain: 'that's agreed'. ·

Unit 19   Look after yourself

1   **Possible answers:**

a) *Toothache*   Take an aspirin and hold some ice in a towel against your face. If the toothache continues for a long time, call the dentist.

b) *Headache*   Take an aspirin and lie down for a while. If the headache continues for a long time, call the doctor.

c) *Nosebleed*   Hold your nose firmly, sit down and lean slightly forward.

d) *Bee sting*   Try to squeeze the sting out. Put a cold, damp towel over the sting to reduce the pain.

e) *Minor burn*   Put the burn under cold water for 10 minutes or until the pain stops. Gently dry it and cover it with a light bandage.

f) *Splinter*   Carefully take the splinter out, wash the finger and then put some antiseptic on. Put a plaster on to keep it clean.

2   Salt – for cleaning cuts; dock leaf – for rubbing on stings; a spider's web – to stop bleeding; camomile tea – to calm someone down; butter – to put on bruises; honey – to put on bruises; a potato – to put on bruises; a piece of beef – to put on black eyes; vinegar – for stings and bruises; lemon – for cleaning and feeling fresh.

Unit 20   The real you

1   **Some example questions:**

What's your name?   What are you doing?   How old are you? When's your birthday?   Do you have any hobbies? What's your favourite colour?   What do you want to be when you grow up? What's your favourite subject at school?   Do you like playing games? Which?   Do you like stories?   What's your favourite story?

2 **Each part of the 'walk in the woods' means something – but don't take it too seriously!**

1   The wood – this is about how you see 'life' in general – happy, busy, active, quiet, stable, etc.

2   The path – this is about how you go through life and how definite you are in your aims.

3   The key shows what you think about material possessions. A key like this means material possessions are important to you:

A key like this means material things are not so important to you:

An old, rusty key means you like artistic things. A new key means you like modern, practical, useful things.

4   The water is your attitude to sex.

5   The house is your attitude to family life.

6/7 The wall (its size, its strength and its condition) is how problems appear to you. What you do about the wall is what you do about problems in general. What you see over the wall is your attitude to 'life after death'.

Unit 12   What's it for?

Notes for Group B
In your group, write three possible uses for each of the two things in your pictures. One of the uses must be the correct one.

a) The correct use:

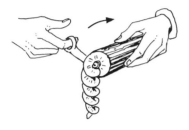

Here are some other possible uses, but you can invent other ones:

b) The correct use:

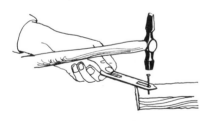

Here are some other possible uses, but you can invent other ones:

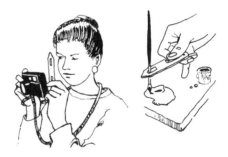

About *Writing 2*

Writing 2 is the second of four writing books in the *Cambridge Skills for Fluency* series. As the approach taken to writing in this and the other three books in the series may be unfamiliar to some teachers and students, the notes which follow outline the basic principles behind the materials and offer some general guidance for their use. These notes are set out under five main questions: Who is *Writing 2* for?; What is the purpose of the book?; How is the book organised?; What kind of activities does the book provide?; and How should the book be used?*

1   Who is *Writing 2* for?

Writing 2 is intended for students with a lower-intermediate knowledge of English who may be studying in language institutes or in the upper classes of secondary schools.

2   What is the purpose of the book?

Writing 2 has two basic aims: firstly, to develop general language proficiency through writing; and, secondly, to develop the skill of writing itself. The first of these aims may seem unusual in 'skills' materials, so some explanation follows.

Writing as a means of developing students' general abilities in English is greatly undervalued in most language courses. Apart from the occasional letter-writing or descriptive paragraph task, general language courses usually restrict writing to tasks such as filling gaps, writing isolated sentences as part of a grammar exercise or doing dictations. Yet there are a number of good reasons for bringing writing into a more central position in classroom work.

   Firstly, in contrast to oral classroom work, writing can offer students the opportunity to work at their own pace and, above all, to think while they are producing language. Many students feel very anxious when they are called upon to speak in front of others and this anxiety effectively blocks their ability to think clearly. Handled correctly, writing can be less stressful. Secondly,

---

* For a fuller account of the rationale behind the book, see the article 'Learning to Write / Writing to Learn' by A. Littlejohn in Les Cahiers des APLUIT 38, Paris, Sept. 1990. The article won first prize in the 1989 English Speaking Union English Language Competition.

writing can give students a chance to retrace their steps, to check and correct what they have written before they are required to show it to another person. This can allow more room for students to develop confidence in their language abilities, to develop their own understanding of how the language works and of what is 'linguistically possible'. Thirdly, unlike oral classroom work, writing can offer a permanent record; students can look back on what they have done, improve, check things, and refresh their memory of what they learnt in class. For these reasons, writing can offer students considerable opportunities to increase their vocabulary, to refine their knowledge of the grammar, and to develop their understanding of how things are best expressed and how well their message is understood. In short, writing can offer more opportunities to learn.

In addition to the potential role of writing in general language development, however, there is also a 'skill' element to be considered – those abilities which are specific to writing itself. There are at least four main aspects to this. Firstly, there is knowledge of the different *types* of writing and the conventions of each (e.g. letters, postcards, messages, notices, reports, poems, etc.). Secondly, there is an understanding of the *function* of a piece of writing and how that is accomplished. Is it intended to amuse? To inform? To persuade? and so on. Thirdly, there is an understanding of the *structure* of a piece of writing. How is the text put together? Is there an introduction? How are examples given? How does the text end? and so on. Finally, there is the matter of the *process* of writing itself. What steps does the writer go through to produce a text? There are probably as many different ways of approaching writing as there are writers, but some common ways one can identify are 'brain-storming' (jotting down points as they occur to you), making and organising notes, writing drafts, revising, writing spontaneously, dictating aloud to oneself, and so on. As far as is relevant for students of General English at this level, the Writing books aim to develop each of these four aspects of writing. Through the Writing books as a whole, students are presented with many types of written text, are asked to consider their purpose and structure and are also introduced to numerous ways in which they can approach their own writing (see question 4 below).

3 How is the book organised?

The book contains 20 units built around different topics. Each unit provides approximately 50–60 minutes of classroom work, although this may vary considerably from group to group and from student to student. The units can be done in any order but you will find that those towards the end of the book tend to demand more from students. Within each unit, there are normally four or five different main activities. You can work straight through a unit from the first activity or, if you prefer, simply choose one or two activities as a supplement to your other work in class. Generally, the activities at the beginning of a unit concentrate on work at the level of vocabulary or sentences, whilst those towards the end of the unit demand paragraph or short 'whole text' writing.

4   What kind of activities does the book provide?

In fulfilling the first purpose of the Writing books − general language development − *Writing 2* aims to provide, as far as is possible, open-ended, creative, imaginative tasks which will stimulate students to use language to say what they wish to say and improve their fluency. You will find, therefore, few exercises with clearly right or wrong answers and few which require students to simply copy or produce 'parallel' texts. Many of the activities are interactive − that is, they require students to write to, for and with other students. The aim in doing this is to encourage students to talk about writing and, thereby, learn from each other. Through working in groups to produce a piece of writing, students have an opportunity to ask each other − and the teacher if need be − about spelling, vocabulary, grammar, and the best ways of expressing things. Interactive writing tasks also give students a unique opportunity to get feedback from their readers on how far their message has been understood and, in so doing, fully integrate writing with the other three main skills − listening, speaking and reading.

As was mentioned above, the second purpose of the books − the development of writing skills − is accomplished by introducing various types of written texts (e.g. letters, postcards, notices, poems), by asking students to consider the purpose of elements of a text, by identifying the structure of a text and by encouraging students to try out different ways in which to approach their own writing. Most of these aspects, however, are not explicitly set out in the materials themselves, although the *Map* at the beginning of the book should enable you to locate a particular aspect of writing should you wish to do so. The aim has been to integrate the various aspects of writing as naturally as possible into the development of a particular topic so that students experience them as 'ways of working' rather than 'things to be learnt'.

In *Writing 2*, particular effort has been taken to develop the range of strategies which students may take in the process of writing. These are offered not as prescriptions but as opportunities to experience and experiment with different ways of going about writing, and the students themselves ultimately make their own decisions about what works best for them as individuals. Below is a list of some of the strategies which are introduced in the book, together with references to example exercises.

− making 'idea maps' (e.g. 1.1)
− making 'word maps' (e.g. 6.1)
− using questions to plan writing (e.g. 1.3, 3.3, 14.4)
− making notes before writing (e.g. 2.2, 8.3, 10.4)
− incorporating reader reactions (e.g. 2.3, 16.2)
− comparing/sharing ideas with others before writing (e.g. 3.3, 5.5, 7.3, 8.2)
− comparing/sharing ideas with others whilst writing (e.g. 2.3, 5.5, 8.3, 10.4)
− 'fluent' writing followed by revising (e.g. 15.1)
− devising correction checklists (e.g. 15.2)

Of the 20 units contained in the book, 13 deal with general topics, five deal primarily with types of written texts (Units 4, 6, 10, 11, 18), and a further two deal with 'learning to learn' topics which encourage students to develop their own ways to help themselves learn (Units 9 and 15). The activities provided in the book range from the light-hearted to the more serious and it is hoped that teachers and students will be able to select units and activities which they find both interesting and useful to do. A concerted effort has been made to devise tasks which draw on students' own experiences and opinions, thereby bringing about more involvement and placing teachers and students on a more equal footing.

5   How should the book be used?

As far as is possible at this level, the instructions for each task are addressed directly to students, making self-access use possible (an *Answer key* is provided to enable students working alone to compare their own answers). Most teachers and students, however, will probably want to make use of the materials in class. It is hoped that the instructions for each task are clear enough to make further, detailed guidance for the teacher unnecessary but some general notes on the use of the materials may, however, be useful.

If you are using the book to support your other classroom work, the *Map* at the beginning of the book will help you find a particular activity. The *Map* shows the main areas of language functions, language structure and vocabulary as well as an indication of the main aspects of writing covered in the units. If, however, you choose to do all of the activities in a unit, you may find it useful to alternate between written work and oral work and, to this end, many of the activities will work just as well as a basis for discussion. The most important thing, though, is that when students are asked to write, they are given time to think, write, revise and discuss with their neighbours and are not unduly rushed. With a class that contains students of varying levels of ability, this may mean that you find that some students finish before others. A useful technique to reduce this problem is to 'chunk' tasks, that is, to ask students to do two or three tasks before they return to whole class discussion. In this way, once students have finished a task, they can move straight on to a further task without waiting for others.

While students are writing, the teacher's job will mainly consist of circulating around the room. The key is for the teacher to be available and not to make students feel defensive of their writing. Writing is unfortunately very commonly used as a means of evaluation, so it is not surprising that many people feel they are being judged when someone reads what they have written. If students do have problems in writing, some teachers find it productive to give hints or clues to students rather than direct answers, since this helps students to develop the ability to write without assistance. It is worthwhile, for instance, keeping a few bilingual dictionaries and grammars available so that students can check things for themselves, without having to ask the teacher all the time. Although this may appear slow and time-wasting, it will help students develop habits which they will almost certainly need when the course is over.

It is often quite useful to provide background music while students are working. This could be classical music, jazz, blues – anything, although it is important to choose something that will not put anyone off. The mood of the music is also significant – if the writing activity involves two stages, one of a group/pair writing and the other of comparison with other groups/pairs, you might choose some calm, relaxing music for the first stage but something more energetic for the second stage.

Many of the activities in the book involve students working in pairs or small groups of three or possibly four students (three is usually the best number as it allows more opportunities for students to contribute their ideas). It is usually best to set a time limit for group work, so that everybody knows how long they have on a particular task before they come together as a class. Since one of the main aims is to develop students' understanding of how English operates, it does not matter too much whether students discuss in English or – with a monolingual group – in their own language. In fact, an 'English only' rule may make communication difficult and thus defeat one of the purposes of group work – to encourage students to help each other and share ideas. The most important thing is that what finally emerges is a piece of written English.

Once the students have written a complete text and they have had an opportunity to discuss and compare ideas, it may be useful to spend some time looking at the *form* of what they have written – that is, the grammar, punctuation, spelling, phrasing and so on. In practice, many of the difficulties which students encounter in writing are often resolved through discussion while they are writing (for example, it is my experience that students frequently correct and revise their own work after having had the opportunity to read and compare with another student's work). Nevertheless, teachers and students may feel it necessary or useful to specifically focus on the accuracy of their writing. This could be done in a variety of ways. Students could, for example, be given some time to look back over their work (in pairs or individually) and to identify any things they are not sure of and which they would like to ask other students or the teacher about. During this time, the teacher could circulate around the class, reading through the students' work. A supply of bilingual dictionaries and grammars would, once again, be useful during this time.

Alternatively, some teachers may prefer to collect in written work for correction. One useful idea for this is to adopt a marking scheme. This involves putting a symbol in the margin indicating the kind of mistake that has been made (e.g. sp = spelling, w/w = wrong word, T = tense, w/m = word missing, w/o = word order is wrong, w/f = wrong form, e.g. 'It were good', ? = I don't understand). This means that students then have to discover for themselves what is wrong, and thus develop the ability to work independently of the teacher.

Writing 2 aims to provide a range of interesting and useful material which will enrich your language course. The tasks aim to bring about more personal involvement on the part of students and give them the opportunity to use English to say what they wish to say. We hope that you enjoy using it.